Emotional Intelligence:
Create the Person You Want to be, Build Confidence, and Develop Your Emotions

The information herein is offered for informational purposes solely and is universal as so. The presentation of the information is without a contract or any type of guarantee assurance.

The trademarks that are used are without any consent, and the publication of the trademark is without permission or backing by the trademark owner. All trademarks and brands within this book are for clarifying purposes only and are the owned by the owners themselves, not affiliated with this document.

Table of Contents

Introduction

You have probably heard the word "intelligence," and maybe you even equate it to someone's education. However, have you heard of "emotional intelligence?" The chances are that you have a vague idea about what this is all about, but if you are lacking in self-confidence or find yourself becoming too emotional in different situations that are presented to you, you are not making the most of the potential of emotional intelligence.

This book was written because I am on a mission. That mission is to help people to gain a better knowledge of what emotional intelligence is all about because it can improve their lives beyond all recognition. We all have emotions. These are the thoughts and the feelings that swing our lives up and down and even find us lost for words or generally lost or confused. However, when you learn to use emotions intelligently, you can actually start to gain confidence and take control of your life. Don't believe me? Then you need to look into the pages of this book, as it may hold answers that you haven't even thought of.

How would I know? I have worked with people from all walks of life and have experienced the mixed bag of emotions that people experience every day of my working life. Having been aware of how people's viewpoints are stilted by their emotions, I thought it a good time to put pen to paper and help those who are finding this particular balancing act hard to control. This is your chance to shine and all you need to do is read and take notice of the chapters that lie ahead. When you do, you will surprise yourself because all you needed was guidance. Taking the right direction gets you there quickly while most people these days seem to prefer their lives to be hit and miss and end up stressed and out of control of their lives. Want all that to change? Then read on, and you will learn how to do just that.

Do try to change things in your way of thinking and use the exercises in the book to help you to do that. Then you will be happier and happier people are more productive and confident people, who give more to their lives and get so much more back.

Chapter One: What is Emotional Intelligence?

When dealing with people, remember you are not dealing with creatures of logic, but with creatures of emotion. -Dale Carnegie

You are probably quite a logical person. You may know what two and two equals, but how emotionally intelligent are you? Do you feel that you are in control of your emotions, or do they sneak up on you when you are not prepared? What about the emotions of other people? Are you capable of handling them and calming situations? If you can do either of these, then you are heading toward emotional intelligence, although many cannot do this balancing act. They are too self-absorbed and let their emotions rule their lives, or they are intolerant of others and lack empathy.

Imagine a manager in a business. He has to have a certain amount of emotional intelligence to be able to get the most from his workforce. That means being able to do the following:

- Able to use active listening
- Able to diffuse difficult situations
- Able to control his own emotions

Bosses who do not possess these abilities are not very good bosses and we all know them. These are people who are too egoist or who don't keep staff very long because their only view toward colleagues is that they are at work for a purpose and nothing else. They forget that people are also human beings with emotional responses. However, when you find entrepreneurs these days that do well for themselves, what you find as well is that colleagues and friends are happy to praise those bosses who inspire them. I remember seeing an article once where people who work with Richard Branson were telling readers about the positive energy they were able to get from his leadership. He himself said in the same interview that he employed people who were energetic and clever because it allowed him to place trust in others who could do specific jobs better than he could. Thus, one can see that emotional intelligence means being able to understand the needs of employees and balance them with the needs of the business. On a personal basis, people who exercise emotional intelligence will show the following traits:

- They will listen to others
- They will know how to empathize
- They are genuine people who can be trusted

There's something else that sets emotionally intelligent people apart from those who do not have this gift. Emotionally intelligent people are aware of their own strengths and weaknesses and can use different emotions to advantage. For example, a poet may be aware that he writes better when he is upset. A mathematician may realize that his powers of analytical investigation are better when he is depressed.

Emotional intelligence helps in so many ways because it makes the path through the maze of life easier and if you can foster this kind of emotional intelligence and make it part of your life, you will not only get on better with people, but you are also likely to put yourself in a direct line for promotion and be able to achieve more than those around you who don't have this gift.

It is not something that gains you qualifications, but it is something that gains you a quality of life. Those who have a high IQ are different from those who have a high level of EI or emotional intelligence and, in the coming chapters, you will be able to test your abilities and try to improve upon them, using your emotional intelligence to help you.

Emotional intelligence keeps you in control of your life in a good way. You will find all the triggers that start your emotions stirring are within your control when you have analyzed them and knew how to control them. The chapters that follow will help you to be able to not only control your emotions but enjoy them as well because you will be more positive in your life and your approach will be very different. In fact, you may enjoy seeing the positive person that you are becoming.

You will learn how to control your emotions and how to judge the emotions of others so that you can respond to them in an appropriate way, instead of letting your emotions take control of you and your potential actions toward others.

Chapter Two: Learning not to Judge

"Whoever undertakes to set himself up as a judge of Truth and Knowledge is shipwrecked by the laughter of the gods." Edmund Burke

During the course of our lives, we tend to judge people because we have a set of standards and these are imposed upon us by our parents and upon them by their parents. Then there are standards set by peers and the standards of society in general. The problem with measuring everything by these standards is that it limits who you are because you are not making a decision based on something that has any solidity. You are basing it upon unwritten rules and that's not a very emotionally intelligent thing to do.

If you want to learn to use your emotional intelligence, you need to be able to let go of judgment and one of the best ways to do this is to learn to meditate. The process of meditation hones in on learning how to let go of thoughts or to see them and not judge them and it's a hard lesson to learn. If you take lessons in meditation or learn to do it yourself, you will find that the mind slows down a little and that when things are said that you would normally judge, you tend to step back a bit from them and don't judge. You simply use the information and quietly deduct whatever you need to in order to help the situation, rather than add complexity to it.

The first place to start is learning to breathe correctly, in through the nostrils and out to a counting system. You count eight as you breathe in and then as you breathe out and as thoughts come to you, you acknowledge them and then dismiss them. They are not appropriate at the time when you are meditating, so you learn to be able to let go of them. If you practice even for as little as fifteen minutes a day, every day, you find that you are not one that judges situations too hastily and this also helps to calm down the emotions and be able to solve things without going through all the negative feelings that people who judge have to endure.

Try it and I am sure that you will find this to be so. Every time that you pass judgment on something, what you are doing is putting up barriers. These barriers make you biased and biased people don't have much emotional intelligence at all. They are too busy building barriers against the world that doesn't fit in with their ideals. The tramp on the corner of the street may just have something valid to say. Don't ignore him because he is a tramp. The preacher in a church may just say something that helps you to see the end to a problem. Even if you are a non-believer, don't put up walls without waiting to hear what is being said. Whenever you do this, you make your emotions snap into judgment mode and that's the unhealthiest state of your mind.

I remember being told that one particular child in a class was trouble. The fact was that the teacher passing this information on wasn't very emotionally intelligent. What the truth of the situation was, as it came to light later, was that she didn't have the teaching abilities to deal with this particular child's problems. Usually, when the pieces don't go together right during the course of your lifetime, there is another reason other than blame and blame doesn't help anyone.

Emotionally intelligent people will be the first to forgive others because they know that circumstances differ for everyone and there may have been reasons why someone did what they did. The world at large is much bigger than what goes on in your head and emotionally intelligent people know this. The reason I suggested meditation as the first step toward emotional intelligence is that it helps you to see things in perspective, slows down your anger and negative feelings and helps you to be able to assess each individual situation using something people don't seem to use much anymore – intuition. When you unlock your intuition, you can trust it because it is there to safeguard you and it helps you to be able to see beyond the obvious.

People who have a high level of emotional intelligence will be calm people who are not quick to judge others, who are able to forgive easily and who understand that their own actions actually dictate the outcome of a situation. They tend not to blame others but instead look into themselves to see what could be done to improve any given situation. That's the difference between them and ordinary people whose level of emotional intelligence is low.

Chapter Three: Connecting the Dots

"Do stuff. Be clenched, curious. Not waiting for inspiration's shove or society's kiss on your forehead. Pay attention. It's all about paying attention. Attention is vitality. It connects you with others. It makes you eager. Stay eager." Susan Sontag

There are times in your life when you feel bad about life or when your emotions go into overdrive. This is quite normal as long as you don't let the emotions dictate the outcome. People who are emotionally intelligent are able to look back at situations that provoked the same kind of emotional response. When they do that, they are also able to see that it was only a matter of time and circumstance that took them out of those negative emotions and back on track. People without emotional intelligence are unable to do that.

For example, if you are drawn to tears of frustration when things go wrong, your mind will analyze the situation and you can join up the dots. You may be saying to yourself that the last time you felt that bad, you managed to move forward by being patient and seeing what the outcome was, rather than assuming the worst. The problem is that people in an emotional state of mind often don't bother to look back and see similar situations where things were solved. They are too busy being unhappy. The emotionally intelligent person knows for example that frustration of this kind triggers an emotional response. They, therefore, understand where the emotional inadequacy comes from and can rationalize it.

The next time that you feel emotional, instead of acting on that emotion, try to analyze it. If you can remember the last time that you felt that way and look at what the outcome was, this helps you to remain focused even though your emotions are trying to take over. Don't let them. You are the driver and when you analyze these things, you make better sense of them. Let me demonstrate.

Kate felt an overwhelming sense of being out of control and was feeling tears running down her cheeks. She could have become even more emotional but chose not to. Instead, she looked at her current circumstances and then looked back to another time in her life when she had felt that bad and was able to see quite clearly that there was a reason for the emotional response. She was then able to calm herself knowing that this response was normal and that there was nothing wrong with her or that response. When you can rationalize your response, it doesn't do as much harm because you don't take it out on the first person that comes along. Instead of doing that, you look inwardly and find your own conclusions.

If you find that you are emotional, try to spend a little more time alone and analyze your feelings and work out why they are happening. The elements to keep out of the picture are:

- Blame
- Jealousy
- Hate
- Anger

These all taint your results. For example, Kate could have blamed her coworker for the way that she was feeling. She could have said that her coworker was throwing too much work at her, but that wasn't, in fact, the case. Although, to an outsider, it may have looked that way, what Kate was actually crying about was that things at home were not the way that she wanted them to be. When she separated these facts from work facts, she was able to get back on track and then tackle the home situation with a fresh outlook, which helped it rather than aggravate it. Someone with less emotional intelligence may have spent the day grumbling about her husband and tried to get people within the office to take sides with her. All this does is fuel a fire and that fire may not actually be necessary. Don't use others to stoke your fires. When you do, things get out of control and your situation becomes worse, rather than better.

If you analyze your feelings, you can then walk away from them because you are able to give them a name or put logic into the situation that doesn't involve others, but merely examines the thoughts and emotions that you have going on in your head and recognizes these from past events. You will then take control of your emotions, knowing and trusting that these negative feelings will pass and that the problem is not as large as your emotional mind is making it out to be.

Chapter Four: Learning to Listen to your Body and Learn to Listen to Others

"Most people do not listen with the intent to understand; they listen with the intent to reply." Steven R. Covey

Although the above quotation relates to talking with someone else, it also applies equally when you talk to yourself. Often you don't listen sufficiently to give reasonable answers and that's where emotional intelligence comes in. When you learn to listen to your body, this means that you are able to slow your life down a little and remember the importance of being aware of how you feel. If you were to stop people in the street and ask how they feel, chances are most people would shrug the question off and ask what you mean. The fact is that there are clues in the messages we receive from our bodies that help us to feel better or to feel more positive, but often we throw the answers at them before we have actually taken the time to be logical and to examine why the body is sending those messages in the first place.

Let me try to examine this in detail so that you can see the sequence of events. If your neck hurts, you may start to feel irritable. You may even shake your head to try to get rid of the ache or swallow a pill hoping that the neck ache will simply vanish. An emotionally intelligent person doesn't tend to do either. They take the time to listen to their body and are able to distinguish from the symptoms what they need to do to ease the pain. Perhaps posture hasn't helped. Perhaps the ache is as a result of sitting in the same position over an extended period. When you don't listen to your body and your aches persist, what happens is that you begin to feel worse and that eventually changes your humor and your emotional wellbeing.

However, if you examine why your body is sending the messages, you can do something tangible about it, so that the body doesn't have to send those messages anymore. For example:

- Change your posture to avoid the pain
- Change your seat, so you don't suffer any more
- Work out what's going on with your body and do something to relieve the pain

Negative people tend to rely on the messages from their body to justify their negativity. However, motivated people with a good sense of emotional intelligence don't do this. They simply work out the problem and do not allow the messages from the body to turn into negative messages that make them feel worse. There's absolutely no benefit to feeling negative about your neck ache. When you feel negative, your emotions jump in and you are snappy and not very nice to be with. When you allow emotional intelligence to step in, you find solutions and thus never reach the point where emotions are able to take over.

It's very much the same when you are listening to people. Really listen. Don't cut into the conversation and assume that what you have to say has more credence than that said by others. When you do, you miss opportunities to get to know people and to learn things. People who do this think very highly of themselves and think their opinions are more important than the opinions of people they are listening to. This makes them emotionally draining. Have you ever met someone who does this? You may know the know-it-all character that visits you and who doesn't listen to anything that you have to say. Do you want people to see you in that way? If not, the only way out of a situation like this is to be patient. Listen with all of your attention. Breathe before you reply. Think out your answers and bear in mind that others are entitled to have different views.

Emotionally intelligent people are those who are open to learning. They not only listen to their own bodies, but they listen to other people and make those around them feel like they are important or liked. That's a very important element because when you stop feeling that way, you actually alienate people and can find that your emotional lows are as a result of your own actions, rather than of the actions of others. Listening to kids can really help you to learn to use your emotional intelligence. Sometimes they come out with amazingly astute ideas that maybe you have left behind you as you have grown up. Embrace the child inside sometimes because we are all entitled to. Those who are able to do this have great imaginations, can see others' points of view and also know that the reason their bodies are complaining is because there is just cause. Emotionally intelligent people find the cause and work on it so that they have a more enriching experience in the future.

If you are not prepared to listen, you will learn nothing at all and your emotional intelligence will be stunted. Hear the laughter of children. Feel the magical feeling of emotional freedom and enjoy experiencing that laughter with someone else who needs it and you will find that your emotional intelligence quota will improve.

Chapter Five: Learning to Gain Confidence

"The most beautiful thing you can wear is confidence." Blake Lively

If you want to gain confidence, emotional intelligence will help you to achieve this. Instead of feeling unsure of your actions and hesitating, hesitate for the right reasons. This hesitation is simply your way of being more certain that the response you give will be one that is considered. Learn to look at your face in the mirror and ask yourself questions that you fear answering. Then, look at the facial expressions that you use when these questions are posed.

The changes in your facial body language come because your emotions kick in whether you want them to or not. Ask people around you questions and you will be able to recognize doubt, lying, unhappiness and all kinds of emotional responses, but that's something that can help you. As you gain confidence in recognizing these things, by using your intuition, you actually start to understand your own reactions better and are able to stem those actions that let you down.

Mary was always upset about the way that people treated her as if she was incompetent. However, when she did this exercise, she suddenly realized that her own reactions were what fueled this opinion in people and she was able to change that. When your emotions turn to confusion or anger, you have a habit of changing your facial expression and your body language. Try it again with the use of a mirror. Shock yourself if you have to because all of this trains you to respond in a different way. When Mary stopped looking in a blank way at people giving her instructions, they started to trust her more with the tasks that they had given her. She was able to develop trusting relationships as well because people didn't know what to make of her expressions and she could see clearly in the mirror what was causing all of this negativity in people who communicated with her.

In fact, you can also make a mental note of times when responses have not been the way you wanted them to be and note down what the questions were and what the responses were so that you are better able to analyze reactions and adjust the way that you put yourself over as a communicator. Look at people who communicate well and who appear to have confidence and their body language is what you need to aim for. The head back, the smile, the shoulders back and the confident stride all help you to be seen as different by others, but they also help you to use your emotional intelligence in a more effective way.

It may be worthwhile keeping a journal. Before you go to bed every night, write out your worries or your doubts and try to come to some kind of conclusion about how you will face them with a smile or at least in a positive way. The things that get in the way of emotional intelligence are:

- Negative thoughts
- Negative self-talk
- Negative emotions

You can look at your own behavior over a given period and try to change your way of handling situations. Instead of negative thoughts, replace them with positive ones. Instead of negative self-talk, start to praise the things that you know you can do well and gradually improve upon the things you find difficult. That feeling that a cyclist gets when he/she first learns to balance on a bike is unforgettable because it's so positive and if you can convert your life into a series of events that all have positive outcomes, you will feel that buzz and people around you will also pick up on your positive energy.

When you find that you are talking negatively to yourself, replace that thought as soon as it comes with breathing exercises that bring you into the moment because these help you to move forward and to realize that you have this habit of talking negatively to yourself. You can even have a song that you can sing quietly in your mind to get rid of these negative thoughts. Emotional intelligence immediately recognizes when a positive input is needed and that's what you are aiming for.

Try and be more empathetic as well. This means being able to place yourself in the shoes of someone else. Instead of thinking negative things about others, try to understand where the negativity or emotional reaction they give comes from and you will find empathy will help you to feel better about them and also about yourself. This helps you to gain confidence and to feel better about being you. Give a beggar a sandwich or try to imagine what it's like for the homeless and do something voluntarily with absolutely no strings attached because when you do, you show your emotional intelligence and will find that voluntary actions actually fuel confidence in yourself.

Conclusion

This is an extremely vast subject, but the way that I have tackled it in this book is intentional. Emotional Intelligence is something you need to measure for yourself and it is only by being aware of your emotions and reading them in different circumstances that you can really get a handle on why you respond in a set way to given circumstance. When you know that, you are less likely to allow emotions to take over and will exercise your emotional intelligence to be able to control negative feelings toward yourself and toward others.

Emotional intelligence helps you to be able to face different circumstances and be able to look beyond the obvious. You will also find that as you meditate on a daily basis, your intuition will truly become honed. There is a very good reason to want to do this as well. Over the course of your life, you have been programmed by everything that happened in your life. If you watch TV, you get programmed into believing that certain products add to your lifestyle. If you watch too much TV of a mindless nature, you tend to become mindless and this exercise once a day will help you to come back into the real world and find the reality of life is actually much simpler than you may imagine.

Being able to read people because of your emotional intelligence also helps them. You will be able to diffuse bad situations and not fall into the trap of letting the emotions take over when there is always some sense of logic behind why everything happens. By analyzing and keeping notes of your emotional responses, you learn to harness the power of emotional intelligence, so that the next time a situation of that nature presents itself, you are ready and able to cope with it.

People say that emotions are there to protect us, although I would say that they are much more than that. They can also destroy us if we let them. However, when you are the driver in your life, rather than allowing your emotions to be just that, you start to see how to use your emotions to help you rather than to work against you. You will understand people better and have a wider perspective on life. You will be able to help people more because your open minded approach means that you have more solutions than most people. You will also find that you get to recognize those emotions that are helping you to grow as a human being and those which can lead to your destruction.

In this day and age, it's even more important that you harness what emotional intelligence you have since more and more people these days are suffering from the effects of stress and it's becoming worse, rather than better. Your emotional intelligence is what brings you back into this moment in time and allows you to see things from a more neutral perspective. You tend to be forward thinking and also know how to respond to people's weaknesses which strengthen you are an individual. You will also be able to recognize the signs of your own emotions trying to take control and will be able to stem them until you have found suitable solutions to your problems. Everyone is born with emotional intelligence. It is only life that takes it away. The way that you were brought up and the circumstances that surround your life play a huge role in how you manage to handle your emotions. When you investigate and start to understand the triggers that make you weaker, you are able to stem emotional overload and become stronger.

I wish you well in your journey and would suggest you read the book several times and implement the suggestions made within its pages if you want to increase your emotional intelligence and start to enjoy your life to the fullest.

Finally, if you enjoyed this book, then I'd like to ask you for a favor, would you be kind enough to leave a review for this book on Amazon? It'd be greatly appreciated!

In order to know when we have new books coming out and well as promotions and discounts, go to http://eepurl.com/coo8z1. We hate SPAM just as much as you do. We will never sell or share your email with anyone.

Thank You

Thank you and good luck!

⇨ To Download Hypnotic NLP: How to Use Hypnosis For Self-Improvement!

⇨ Go to: **https://tinyurl.com/ydf3eylg**

In this Ebook, you are about to Discover...

- 10 Steps to Attract the Life You Want

- Using NLP to Overcome Mental Barriers

- Using NLP to Overcome Procrastination

- Using NLP in Developing Attraction

- Using NLP in Wealth Manifestation

-   How to Use NLP to Overcome Social Phobia

-   Using NLP to Boost Self-Confidence

-   Using NLP as a Model of Communication with Others

-   Master NLP in 5 East Steps

-   Much, Much More!

Hurry, Download this Ebook for a limited time! Maximize your life!

Check Out More Great Content!

Search on Amazon: Andrew Anxiety

Search on Amazon: Andrew NLP

Search on Amazon: Andrew Intermittent Fasting Beginner's

Preview Of "Anxiety: What is Anxiety and Simple Ways to Reduce Anxiety, Social Anxiety, Panic Attacks, and Fear in Order to Master Your Life" By: Andrew Kuehn

Is It Stress or Anxiety Disorder?

Most people tend to confuse normal anxiety, or stress, with anxiety disorder. They are two totally different things. Here are just a few examples to help you understand the differences:

- With stress, you worry about your bills, lack of a job, or getting dumped by your girlfriend. Once the stressor or trigger is taken away, you stop worrying. With an anxiety disorder, you are constantly worried about these things for no reason at all. You find yourself undergoing daily distress even though the stressor has disappeared.

- Stress is where you go to a social gathering and start feeling self-conscious or uncomfortable, maybe because of the way you are dressed. With an anxiety disorder, you totally avoid any kind of social gathering because you are afraid of being humiliated or embarrassed in some undefined way.

- Stress is what you feel before you sit for an exam, give a presentation, or attend an interview. A stressor is a significant event that can impact your life. Anxiety disorder, however, is where you experience a sudden overwhelming fear for no reason at all, and you live in perpetual dread having another panic attack.

- Stress involves a rational fear of what you consider a dangerous situation, place, or object. Once you leave the place or eliminate the threatening object, you become okay. With an anxiety disorder, you find yourself afraid of things that are non-threatening, and even though the object is removed, you remain terribly afraid.

- Stress is what you experience immediately after a traumatic event, for example, when you avoid a car collision. You may find it difficult to sleep after such a situation. However, an anxiety disorder is where you have recurring flashbacks or nightmares of the accident some months or even years after the event.

Experts are still learning more about anxiety disorders. They have found that it can actually run in families and has some sort of biological basis. So far, what we are sure of is that anxiety disorders are a result of a complex combination of risk factors that include genetics, personality, brain chemistry, and events you experienced in your life.

Want more? Type B074R5YJND into the search bar on Amazon.